AL FRESCO

Fougasse

Edited with an introduction by
BEVIS HILLIER

ELM TREE BOOKS · LONDON

The publishers gratefully acknowledge the
co-operation of the proprietors of *Punch*, who
retain the copyright of the majority of the drawings
in this book; The Imperial War Museum; London
Transport; Mr Peter Dickinson, and especially
Mrs Mollie Bird without whose help and enthusiasm
this book would not have been published.

First published in Great Britain 1977
by Elm Tree Books/Hamish Hamilton Ltd
90 Great Russell Street, London WC1B 3PT

Introduction © 1977 by Bevis Hillier

ISBN 0 241 89462 X

Printed in Great Britain by
Butler & Tanner Ltd, Frome and London

introduction

IN THE EARLY 1920s readers of *Punch* began to notice the cartoons of an artist who had made his first appearance in the magazine during the First World War. His style was developing rapidly into a kind of minimal art. His comic subjects were rendered with extreme economy, in jaunty, jerky lines: someone said he drew as a canary might draw if it could. He signed himself 'Fougasse'. Was he, some wondered, a Frenchman, imported because our own cartoonists were not funny enough? But if so, how had he gained such an intimate knowledge of English sports?

In fact he was a young Englishman, who only lately had been doing all his work flat on his back or propped up on seven pillows: his spine had been fractured by a Turkish shell at Gallipoli. His real name was Cyril Kenneth Bird, but as there was already a *Punch* artist who signed himself 'W. Bird' (some thought it was the *nom de plume* of Jack B. Yeats, the poet's brother) he chose a pseudonym. A 'fougasse' was a French mine, a rough and ready affair which might or might not go off: Kenneth Bird modestly thought the same was true of his cartoons.

He was born on 17 December 1887, at 26, Westbourne Terrace Road, London, the son of Arthur Bird, who was in the wine trade in a gentlemanly kind of way, but was better known as an England cricketer and a first-class shot. Kenneth disliked shooting because he loved animals and birds; later he designed many posters and pamphlets for wild-life organizations.

He attended Warwick House (day) school from 1893 to 1898; boarded at Farnborough Park School, Hampshire, from 1898 to 1902; and in 1902 went to Cheltenham College, where he became head boy at the early age of 16. He was outstanding academically, but told his father he wanted to be an artist. His father said that he would not be rich enough to 'keep' him: he must train for a job. So he studied engineering at King's College, London. He arrived there in 1904 and became President of the University Union Society and of the Engineering Society. He also played rugby and boxed for the college.

5

His friend Donald McCullough wrote to *The Times** after his death: 'He continued to play rugby and in 1913 in the final international trials he scored the only try. He would have been certain of his Cap for Scotland but he got concussion and remained unconscious until the match was over.' Rugby was a lifelong interest, and he designed many posters and illustrated several booklets for the Rugby Football Union.

Kenneth found time also to attend classes at the Regent Street Polytechnic and at the School of Photo-Engraving and Lithography in Bolt Court. He was also a machine-gun instructor in the Artists' Rifles. One of his contemporaries at King's was Lieutenant-Colonel R. S. Timmis, DSO, who after Fougasse's death recalled his friend in *The King's Engineer* (the magazine of the King's College Engineering Society), volume 43. His most vivid memory was of a 'screamingly funny lunch' at Kenneth's club: 'all the waiters gathered round the table, and were in fits of laughter'.

Kenneth graduated B.Sc. in Civil Engineering in 1908. In that year he was sent to Spain by the Steel Company of Scotland to survey iron mines. In 1909 he joined Easton, Gibb & Son at Rosyth, the naval base outside Edinburgh. It was while working there that he met his future wife, Mary ('Mollie') Holden Caldwell. She was staying nearby with her aunt and uncle. An old admiral at the base wrote to the aunt and uncle saying 'I know you have quite a lot of nieces. Could you ask some of my boys over?' Mary Caldwell's aunt asked five of them to dinner – among them, Kenneth Bird. Fougasse's widow recalls: 'One of the young men had the most terrible smell of mothball on his dinner clothes. We were all too polite to say anything about it. But then my uncle came in and said "Oh, what a *hell* of a smell!"''

She was much taken with Kenneth, with his sportsman's bearing and acute brown eyes. On a later visit, he asked what she called a pet monkey she then had. 'I said, "I call him Kenneth." He couldn't help laughing. He said, "I know perfectly well why you called him Kenneth. Because I've got beady brown eyes."' In October, 1913, Mollie's father, who could see the way things were going, held out half-a-crown to Kenneth and said: 'I bet you half-a-crown she won't accept you by Christmas.' Kenneth won his half-crown. He and Mollie were married at St Matthew's, Bayswater, on 16 September 1914 by the Rev. C. H. Wilson, vicar of Marchwood, a cousin of the bridegroom.

Kenneth's father-in-law, William Hay Caldwell, was a remarkable man. A Fellow of Gonville and Caius College, Cambridge, he was elected to a Royal Society travelling scholarship in 1883 and used it to go to Australia to research whether duck-billed platypi were egg-bearing or gave birth direct to baby platypi. He was the first to establish conclusively that platypi bore eggs. After that he virtually abandoned zoology and became a paper manufacturer in his native Scotland. He was the type of the eccentric and venturesome Victorian scientist as portrayed by Conan Doyle and H. G. Wells. At Morar Lodge in Scotland, the house he rented from his friend Lord Lovat, he occupied himself with inventions for increasing the sensitivity of photographic emulsions; with the 'chemistry of digestion'; and the problem of vaporizing heavy oils for internal combustion engines. Kenneth, who was always interested in technical questions, corresponded with him a lot and made suggestions which Caldwell found helpful. Can it have been mere coincidence that when the *Daily Herald* of 24 May 1922 reviewed Fougasse's book *Gallery of Games* it commented: 'This book contains some 50 cartoons

* *The Times*, 18 June 1965.

on every sport except hunting the platypus, and that of course is not humorous – for the platypus'?

By the time of his marriage, Kenneth was a second lieutenant in the Royal Engineers. He flouted the stern tradition of that corps: 'Majors may, captains should not, lieutenants *must not*, marry.' At the time, Kenneth and his friends were working on submarines at Rosyth. This work was of enough importance to prevent their being sent abroad at once. Eventually Kenneth's friends were sent out to France, but he could not go because a dentist in Southsea had pulled out his tooth but left in the stump, which became infected. His temperature rose to 106. William Caldwell, with whom they were staying, was very concerned and summoned the doctor. Mollie Bird recalls: 'I had the pleasure of holding Kenneth's head while the doctor pulled out the stump. He said "I can't possibly give any anaesthetic with that temperature."' In a week, Kenneth was well again. He was sent to Gallipoli with the 52nd Division in 1915.

He was blown up by a shell. His wife received a 'very tactful letter' from his general. Its substance was: 'I can't say what is going to happen; but you'll get your husband home.' Mollie Bird realized that they thought he would not live. She went to see him in hospital in Vincent Square. He could not speak. When eventually he came home, 'all he said to me – it took a lot of time – was, "Don't you feel cold without me?"'

They moved into a flat of her parents in Chelsea. A roof over their head was about all they had. The Caldwells were quite wealthy but they did not realize that Kenneth was not. Before her marriage, Mollie was given an allowance of £300 a year to buy nice clothes. This came to an end when she married. 'My mother didn't realize our situation. When she did finally realize how poor we had been, she said: "You little pig! Why didn't you tell me?"'

It was obvious that Kenneth could not return to engineering. It was equally obvious that they could not live in any comfort on his meagre pension from the army. His first thought was to write short stories. These were sent back with rejection slips. 'The stories were worse than there was any need for them to be,' he later recalled in a characteristic turn of phrase. He turned from writing to drawing. From a child he had been an accomplished artist. Mrs Bird still preserves a small watercolour of red roofs which Kenneth painted at the age of seven. Visitors to her house at Forres, Inverness, today cannot believe that it was the work of a child. At Christmas 1900 his father had given him a little sketch-book bound in green and maroon leather stamped with gold fleurs-de-lys. In it he had drawn several ink cartoons which already show something of his later genius for hitting off a scene in a few vital, squiggly lines: 'A Suggestion for Waits: a Patent Bomb-Proof Shelter'; 'A Brilliant Charge by the Artists'; and some of the current jokes about the Boer War – 'Q. Why are our soldiers in S. Africa never dry? A. Because of The Wet (DeWet)' or 'Q. Why do not the Boers wear stockings? A. Because we have given them socks.' The book also contained some of his early rugby jokes: 'Backs and Half Backs' was a Phil May-like drawing of the backs of a man in a brown derby hat, a woman in a long dress and picture hat, and a small boy in a wideawake; while 'Linesman' was cunningly rendered in straight lines. Even more anticipatory of the mature Fougasse were pictorial comedies divided into episodes. Thus The Tourist first packs up; then goes away, muffled in tartans in his quilted railway compartment; then arrives at his destination with a servant pushing a huge barrow of luggage behind him; then sets to work, painting a picture; then returns in a

horse-cab. In each scene, within the limits of his nurseling talent, Bird managed to extract the maximum of comedy from the situations which were then commonplace, simply by pointed observation. Another Fougasse trick of later years, also seen here in infancy, is the historical retrospect: a series of 'Duels' takes us from knights in armour through to pistols at dawn. Characteristic Fougasse touches are the 'Keep off the Grass' sign over which two pigtailed bravos are duelling with rapiers, and the tall-hatted umpire in the pistol duel shouting 'Demi Temps!' (Half-time). The drawings show the influence of Phil May and of Caran d'Ache both in the economy of line and in the episodic method favoured by Caran; though a paragraph in *The Star* of 27 January 1923, suggested another possible exemplar for the episodic manner:

> Mr. Joseph Priestman Atkinson, who has just died at his home in Crescent Grove, that old-world backwater which faces the south side of Clapham Common, was the last surviving member of the staff of *Punch* when Mark Lemon edited it. Mr. Atkinson's most notable contribution to *Punch* was the 'Dumb Crambo' series of thumbnail sketches. They introduced the idea of a continuous story told in small sketches which Mr. Bateman* and Fougasse are popularising in *Punch* now.

The scene of 'Polo' from a series on 'Roman Sports' in Bird's juvenile sketchbook is not the funniest, but it is the most accomplished of the sketches –

* i.e. H. M. Bateman (1887–1970): see p. 17.

amazing work for a youth of 20 (he signed it in full and dated it 1907). It shows that Bird already had the gift of capturing movement in line, on which the *Manchester Guardian* of 2 May 1922 was to comment when reviewing his book *Gallery of Games*: 'It is an interesting proof of the superiority of the artist over the machine that the figures of these sportsmen, as drawn by "Fougasse", are moving more rapidly over their printed page than any creatures of the kinema.'

In 1912, Bird drew and painted 'The Life Class' – two artists painting a cherub perched on top of a column. In 1913 he drew and coloured the delightful 'Stained Glass window designed while waiting for the postman', showing the postman in his uniform and old shako divided up into lozenges of azure and or, with vert trees behind and an unfinished gules pillar-box. On the back of the piece of Bristol board on which this was executed, he painted a shiny shoe kicking a tube of Chinese white into infinity, with the caption 'Banished'. This was symbolic of his move towards a cleaner, crisper kind of drawing in which highlights would be suggested by expert penmanship, not by blobs of Chinese white. He told an interviewer that he used the rubber more than the pencil; but his widow told me: 'He never made messes. He was wonderfully neat in everything he did. But he didn't draw the final cartoon straight off. He did dozens of sketches until he'd got it right.' As well as eliminating superfluous lines from his drawings, he also eventually discarded the old laborious 'Stout Party' captions of which the drawing was merely an illustration; he believed in getting as much of the joke as possible into the cartoon itself.

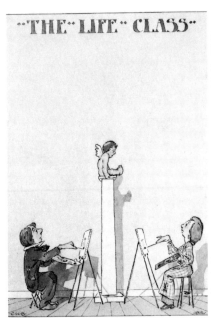

Precocious as he was, Fougasse needed tuition. In 1916 he decided to take a correspondence course in illustration from the Press Art School, Forest Hill, which Percy V. Bradshaw had founded in 1905. An advertisement which Bradshaw put into *Punch*, 17 February 1926, when Fougasse had become one of his star pupils, conveys the tone of the school:

I want to talk quietly and sincerely to those young men and women who are finding that Wireless, Pictures, Dancing and so on, all good and entertaining in their way, do not give *quite* the return in self-improvement and joy that a Hobby should.

To them I suggest Drawing. There is no Hobby to equal it. Its cost is very little – *an important point when choosing a Hobby*. And, as one progresses, it is found that subjects producing joy and interest abound – sheerly abound, in winter's snow and summer's shine alike.

Bradshaw further claimed: 'I have taught drawing by post to several thousands of people since 1905 when I started the Press Art School. Many of the leading illustrators of today are my old pupils. Upwards of a thousand sketches by old pupils have appeared in *Punch* alone.'

Stained Glass window – designed while waiting for the Postman   *Cuss. '13*

Fougasse's first cartoon in *Punch* appeared in the issue of 16 July 1916. Signed 'Fougasse', it was called 'War's Brutalising Influence'. It comprised two drawings. The first showed a young officer whose immaculate, dandified uniform is straight out of a military outfitter's catalogue. The drawing is prissy and stilted to match. In the second sketch, which is executed with panache and melodramatic chiaroscuro, the prim young officer has changed into a jutting-jawed, pipe-smoking veteran whose uniform has evidently seen active service. The drawing was accepted by F. H. Townsend, the brilliant illustrator of an 1890s collected edition of Thomas Love Peacock's novels, who had been appointed the first art editor of *Punch* in 1905. Townsend, who shared with the *Punch* artist H. M. Brock the peculiarity of drawing with his left hand but writing with his right, was a friendly patron to Fougasse, but died in 1920, when Frank Reynolds, even more convinced of Fougasse's talent, succeeded to the post.

At first Fougasse drew heavily on his war service for subjects. In one of his early drawings, an indignant kilted Highlander, purple with rage, has encountered the inscription 'Gott strafe England' scrawled on a wall. Fougasse has made him cross out 'England' and substitute 'Great Britain'.

SCOTLAND FOR EVER.

Another is of the 'bashful VC' who returns to the trenches, with shells exploding all around, rather than face the Mayor and reception committee in his home town. A third, entitled 'The Making of History', shows an unimpressive officer buying a German helmet as a souvenir in 1915, and the gradual accretion of heroic fictions about his exploits in obtaining it, until in 1970 he is claiming to have cut off the head of a general who was wearing it.

As British interest in the war years faded, Fougasse turned his attention to social life in Britain, in particular the social life of the upper middle classes, to which he and his wife belonged and for whom *Punch* was still largely produced. As his cartoons always relied more on telling observation than on exaggeration, his drawings are a vivid pictorial chronicle of 'U' Britain between the Great War and the mid-1950s. It is a world where men wear plus-fours for golf and dress for dinner, grappling in Laocoönish writhings with refractory bow ties and shirt-fronts; where clubs are still preserves of glowering masculinity; where public school blazers and the Flag still matter. Suffering is being made to walk to the front of the taxi rank, or mistaking a traffic cop for someone's chauffeur. Railway carriages are still luxurious padded cells, peopled by amiable lunatics. The wireless is a noisy novelty. Blocks of flats and neon lighting annoy us slightly in the late 1920s. Changing our room décor to harmonize with the new Art Deco cushion is fraught with aesthetic perils. Horrors such as the reversible suit and the spivs impinge on us in the late 1940s, after all those wartime queues; but the world wags on much as before, and there's still a good market for yet another reprint of that funny book on contract bridge, first published in 1934.

Both Fougasse's improvement as an artist and his rise to popularity were extraordinarily rapid. A. E. Johnson wrote in December 1921: 'It is less than four years since the first Fougasse drawings appeared, and seldom, if ever, has a humorous artist made good with the public in so brief a space of time.' Apart from his regular contributions to *Punch*, two things in particular helped to make his reputation: the annual *Punch* almanacks, and the collections of his cartoons published in book form early in his career. On 29 November 1919, the *Ladies' Friend*, commenting on *Punch Almanack* for 1920, said: 'The strike spirit is delightfully parodied by "Fougasse" in his tour "Unrest through the Ages" – the staff of the Borgias demanding board wages, and Canute's controversy with the mariners are treated with a real spirit of humour.' The *Morning Post* of 11 May 1920 spoke approvingly of 'funny Mr. Fougasse' who had suggested ways in which the 'pictorial and plastic *drolatiques*' of contemporary art could be put to good use, in a series called 'A Use for Modern Art'.

His first book, *A Gallery of Games*, originally published by Jonathan Cape in 1921, was republished by Methuen in 1922. The drawings were still those of a good amateur; perhaps the best is of the billiard player whose cigar ash lengthens, frame by inexorable frame, until it finally drops on the green baize of the table, to the fury of his host, who poniards him with a cue. *A Gallery of Games* had a dull preface by E. V. Lucas; but Fougasse's next book, *Drawn at a Venture* (1922) was most wittily introduced by A. A. Milne, who remarked that Fougasse's cartoons 'make the very jokes which we should have made for ourselves, if only we had realised that they were jokes'. Milne was a great friend of the Birds: Mollie Bird recalls that on the night Christopher Robin was born, Alan Milne wrote her a four-page letter about the event.

In 1924, Fougasse was famous enough to be asked to design a miniature book for Queen Mary's Dolls' House, to which Max Beerbohm and A. A.

QUEST

TRAGEDY OF A CIGAR-ASH.

Milne also contributed. Fougasse's miniature, which E. V. Lucas considered the best thing in the dolls' house library, was an illustrated verse fairy tale called *J. Smith*: Fougasse contributed the verse as well as the drawings. He was also beginning to get a lot of advertising work, including the commission for an L.N.E.R. railway poster designed in 1925, of which the *Daily Telegraph* of 26 May 1925, said: 'Fougasse has succeeded in executing that rare thing, a humorous poster, although the eccentric figure stretching out of a carriage window to breathe the early-morning air of Scotland, is transgressing all the company's by-laws.' Fougasse also designed posters for the London Underground, including one praised by the *Morning Advertiser* of 18 April 1925, which showed a sectional view of a London street and the tube tunnels below: the caption suggested that above ground there was 'too much waiting and too little room', while below ground there was 'plenty of room and no waiting'. Among his early patrons were Abdullah Cigarettes, for whom he designed several cartoon-advertisements. Later he drew a very successful series for Pyramid Handkerchiefs, in which handkerchiefs, twisted and tweaked into cartoon figures, take energetic part in sports.

The Birds were now making a comfortable living from art. Mollie Bird was an artist too; she made limpid, Japanesey watercolours of the rocky landscape around her home at Morar, Inverness. A Bond Street dealer who came to buy from Kenneth in 1921 said he would like to buy her work too. On several occasions, Kenneth and Mollie held exhibitions together: when they held one at the Fine Art Society, London, in 1926, *Punch* (5 May) called them 'Fougasse and Fougassine'. Besides the Milnes, who lived near them in Chelsea Manor Street, their friends included the cartoonist Lewis Baumer and [Sir] Owen Seaman, with whom they spent three holidays in the north and south of France and Monte Carlo. Seaman contributed verses about these holidays to *Punch* of 25 March 1925 and 16 April 1929, dedicating them to Kenneth and Mollie. This is a sample of the second of the verses:

> The franc's vagaries may have left me stoney,
> And yet, this hour, I'd blow my final sou
> To see the palms of Menton (or Mentone),
> The towering palms that fringe her tideless blue;
> To climb the hill where Paynim loved to harry
> Old Eze's walls; or in your sporting car
> To mount the way – a careless *partie-carrée* –
> That winds to Castellar.

And he dedicated to Mollie verses in the issue of 3 November 1926, on a temptation he had resisted to say 'Good-night, Mollie' at the end of a BBC talk on 'Humour'.

In 1933 Kenneth and Mollie both became Christian Scientists. Neither enjoyed good health. The late Christopher Hollis, himself a Roman Catholic, wrote in his memoirs *The Seven Ages* (1974):

I had never previously met Kenneth Bird, though, of course, like everybody else, I was well acquainted with his delicate and witty drawings. Naturally, sitting next to him each week [at the *Punch* Table, of which Hollis became a 'member' in Malcolm Muggeridge's editorship] I had the opportunity of getting to know him very well and seldom have I met anyone for whom I had a higher admiration. He had been badly wounded in the First World War and ascribed his wholly unexpected recovery to a miracle. This miracle was, he believed, due to his faith in Christian Science, of which he was a fervent disciple and to which he devoted his life. . . . Kenneth Bird never made any attempt to convert me or, as far as I observed, anybody else to Christian Science. He went down every week to Eton to give a voluntary instruction to the boys of his faith. . . . His own conversation and conduct were models of kindness and charity. Brimful as he was of wit, I never heard him say a wounding word about anybody. . . .

Kenneth was indeed deeply serious about his religion; but Mollie Bird has an amusing anecdote about his early days in the faith. She attended the Christian Science church in Curzon Street with him. Halfway through the service, people were encouraged to stand up and talk about the illnesses they had been cured of. One old woman stood up and said she was so grateful to the Christian Science church because it had taught her to mind her own business. As Mollie and Kenneth were walking to the Ritz afterwards, he commented: 'It must be a marvellous religion, if it teaches old women to mind their own business.'

In 1937 Fougasse became Art Editor of *Punch*. He restyled the magazine and improved its typography. He gave great encouragement to a new breed of young artists who were to become the leading *Punch* illustrators of the 1950s. One of them was Rowland Emett, whose first attempt was sent back with a 'Not bad. Try again.'

With the outbreak of war in 1939, Fougasse offered his services free of charge to any ministry who wished him to design posters. E. J. Embleton, studio manager at the Ministry of Information, wrote to him on 3 November 1939: 'Dear Fougasse, I felt I would like to thank you for your kindness in offering to design some anti-rumour posters for us at such short notice.' The posters for which Fougasse is perhaps better remembered than for any of his purely comic work, are the 'Careless Talk Costs Lives' series, which showed Hitler and Goering materializing in the unlikeliest places. But he also designed a wide variety of other propaganda posters, exhorting people to save paper, send books to the Forces or join the different training corps. Mollie Bird recalls that the Air Force security was so slapdash that Kenneth made a formal protest; the Army was quite good; while the Navy was so concerned about security that the officer who brought papers for Kenneth to translate into illustration kept his hand on them while Kenneth made sketches. 'I had to keep my eyes closed while drawing,' as Kenneth dryly remarked.

In many cases he was giving pictorial clarity to complicated technical points. A letter from the Signal Department, Admiralty, dated 19 November 1941 reads:

My dear Bird,

Many thanks for your sketches. The Signal Department has laughed a good deal and I am sure the Fleet will do likewise. You have invited me to criticize, so here goes. A, B, C, D & E: perfect just as they stand. F: suggest deleting the flag and retaining the American rating's cap only. G: do not forget that submarines frequently rest on the bottom, particularly in shallow water. What about making the Mariner's Rest on the bottom of the sea with appropriate fishes and mermaids? H: a search-light is more frequently used for this type of signalling. When so used it is fitted with a square contraption on the front which, after a handle is pressed down on the side, opens a series of shutters like a Venetian blind. What about making him an American sailor?

Yours ever, John Buist.

while, finally, in .0002 per cent. it was
due to someone's carelessness.

Both Kenneth and Mollie served as air-raid wardens – a task which gave him material for several cartoons about the Blackout, and for the entertaining series of excuses made by people who allowed light to show at their windows ('In 5 per cent of the cases examined, it was owing to having just moved in that day.... In 12 per cent it was my daughter's room, and she's only here occasionally') which he illustrated in *Family Group*, a book published in 1944.

In 1949, on the retirement of his friend E. V. Knox ('Evoe') as Editor of *Punch*, Fougasse accepted the post – with genuine reluctance. 'I'd much rather not,' he said; but the Agnews, proprietors of the magazine, persuaded him to take on the job for a short time. On 14 December 1948, after the appointment had been announced, he wrote to the design historian and novelist John Gloag:

Dear Gloag,
How very good of you to wire.
I value your kind wishes very much indeed, and shall need them quite a lot. I keep on telling myself that it's going to be fun in many ways, without, so far, entirely convincing myself; but I'll keep at it.
Again, with very much gratitude,
Yours very sincerely,
Kenneth Bird.

Fougasse was only the seventh editor of *Punch* since the magazine was founded in 1841, and the first to have drawn his way to the editorial chair. He took over on All Fools' Day, and to mark the event gave the *Punch* cover (still the old Dicky Doyle design of the 1840s) a red border, while Mr Punch blossomed surprisingly in the colours of the Brentford Football Club and Toby was given a raspberry-coloured ruff. Inside, the old Garamond italic type gave way to Studio as the bridge between the old type face and the new one for future numbers designed by Milner Gray.

Though Kenneth was popular among the staff, it was not felt that he was happy in the editorship. His interest was in art and technical matters; he left the choice of writers almost entirely to H. F. Ellis, a double-First from Oxford who had the title Literary Editor. Kenneth's aim was to keep *Punch* as the British tradition it had been for so long. He ran it in the old gentlemanly way, coming in only on Tuesdays, Wednesdays, and Thursday mornings. True, he was anxious to recruit bright young writers and artists with no previous experience, graduates whom he could mould to the magazine's character. But the method of recruitment was the old courtly method. He wrote to a don at Cambridge to ask for suitable people, while Humphry Ellis wrote to an Oxford don. The writer Peter Dickinson, who was a protégé of Kenneth's, said, 'I was the only candidate in my year. Kenneth had written to his Cambridge don, who had suggested me; but Humphry had forgotten to write to his Oxford don.' When Malcolm Muggeridge took over from him as Editor in 1953, he was, Dickinson says, 'bowled over by the level of inexperience of the staff, and their lack of contact with the outside world'.

B. A. Young, who wrote for Kenneth Bird, recalls him as a rather withdrawn, quiet man, who as a Christian Scientist did not drink or smoke or join the staff on their outings to Fleet Street pubs. He also remembers his altering the title he had given one piece – 'Country Matters' – as too risqué for *Punch*. Where Kenneth most impressed him was in editorial conferences, at which 'he was able to produce the most astonishingly good rough drawings at a moment's notice. He would draw a dog baying at the moon in a matter of seconds. If you were lucky, you could collect his sketches after the conference.' Fougasse was in charge of the two special issues published to celebrate the Festival of Britain (1951) and the Coronation (1953), for both of which he designed delightful covers – the Festival one an impish parody of Abram Games's Festival symbol, which Fougasse converted into a kind of grinning starfish. Perhaps the best effects of his editorship were his patronage of Emett and of Ronald Searle, a brilliant young artist still in his twenties.

He retired in 1953 but continued to draw for the magazine. He also wrote several books, including *The Good-Tempered Pencil* (1956), a survey of cartoon art in which, characteristically, he included not a single drawing by himself. He died in 1965. A memorial exhibition of his work was held in the following year at the Fine Art Society.

Fougasse always maintained that a man with a good sense of humour but not particularly gifted as a draughtsman was far more likely to make a good cartoonist than a talented artist with a poor sense of humour. Though he was finally able to temper his style into an impressive and unique instrument of visual satire, Fougasse belonged more to the first category than to the second. His draughtsmanship did not compare in energy or invention with that of his chief *Punch* rival, H. M. Bateman, although Mollie Bird stoutly maintains that it was Fougasse who first drew a cartoon in the series 'The Man Who . . .' which established Bateman's reputation, and that Bateman 'borrowed' the idea. His merit was to devise irresistible jokes and to put between them and the reader's appreciation of them, the minimum barrier of lines.

Like any humorist, he developed various set techniques for making people laugh. In the episodic cartoons, his most common effect is a cumulative joke ending in explosive climax or equally melodramatic bathos. The cigar ash on the billiard table is one example of the climactic joke; another is the after-dinner speaker who sits in mute but growing fury as a classic bore introduces him, and finally stabs the tormentor with a table knife and leaps out of the

THE MAN WHO SNEEZED

window. A splendid example of anti-climax, perfectly timed, is the pictorial dissertation on taxi windows. Some are shut and won't open. Some are open and won't shut. The third series shows those which move perfectly freely. Only in the last frame of all do we get the pay off: the free-moving window falls right out and smashes into splinters.

The Aeroplane of 15 April 1925 described one of the cumulative Fougasse cartoons ending in bathos to illustrate a point about aviation:

> Some time near the end of the war in 1918, *Punch* . . . published a picture by the inimitable Fougasse, showing first a British soldier in ordinary service kit. In the next picture, a hand is holding out to him a tin hat or 'battle bowler'. In the next picture he appears in a tin hat and a hand is presenting to him a coil of barbed wire. In the next picture the hand is giving him a basket of carrier pigeons – and so on for about six or eight pictures till the unfortunate soldier is seen staggering along with bent knees under the burden of his equipment. In the last picture one sees a German's head on the horizon, all the official gadgets strewn around in the foreground, and Mr. Thomas Atkins prancing into action, bareheaded and in his shirtsleeves, armed solely with a rifle and a bandolier.
>
> Something very like that is what happens to officially hampered aircraft on active service. . . .

The multiplication of objects also amused Fougasse hugely. A man entering a hatter's piled to the ceiling with hats, mumbles: 'Have you any—er—hats?' Outside a ballroom, the grand, richly carpeted stairs are littered with a thousand hastily stubbed-out cigarette-ends. Wireless aerials form a spiky imbroglio of lines against the night sky above the caption: '*Now* who says that we're not a musical nation?' Looking up at the myriad windows of a Grand Hotel, a cloche-hatted woman says to her husband: 'Oh, Percival, how dreadful! When I sent that picture postcard to Aunt Louisa, I do believe I put a cross against the wrong window.'

" HAVE YOU ANY—ER—HATS ? "

The absent-minded Gentleman: "IT'S QUITE ALL RIGHT, CONSTABLE. I AM WELL AWARE THAT THIS IS ONLY A DREAM. I ASSURE YOU THAT I FREQUENTLY EXPERIENCE THIS TYPE OF NIGHTMARE."

The Odd Man Out is one of his favourite characters, whether he is wearing Oxford bags when the fashion has not yet caught on, or still sporting them when the fashion has passed. We are intended to be sympathetic towards him when he is the gallant 'little 'un' opposing his puny independence against the mighty (like the skipper of the tiny sail-boat who assures his distraught passenger, as the hulk of a huge liner looms above them, 'It's quite all right, my dear fellow. You see, everything has to give way to a sailing-vessel.') We are still intended to feel sympathy for him, but of another kind, when he is an absent-minded professor who has come out without his trousers, assuring a policeman as vast crowds and traffic jams pile up as far as the eye can see: 'It's quite all right, Constable. I am well aware that this is only a dream. I assure you that I frequently experience this type of nightmare.' Sometimes the little man does what we have all thought of doing, but never dared to: like 'The Man who Couldn't Get Attention' who steals a figurine in a department store and is at once pounced on by hordes of ravening assistants. Just a few of the jokes depend on colour, such as the tragedy of Mr Botticelli Binns who devoted so much thought to the repainting of his house (blancmange pink, green and blue) before he heard of the proposal to erect a new pillar-box in front of it.

Fougasse's style was already assured and idiosyncratic by the time his three large-format books were published – *P.T.O.* (1926), *E.&.O.E.* (1928) and *Fun Fair* (1934). But to my mind his hieroglyphic, almost notional style was not fully-fledged until the Second World War. It was perhaps the need to get across his message in the most unambiguous way that forced him to prune and pare down to the quintessence of his figures: as it were, the pipe-cleaner embedded in the soft toy.

Max Beerbohm had said with flippant callousness in the 1930s: 'We need another war, to bring out the best in our artists and kill off the worst of them.' Fougasse, who had suffered so much in the First World War, benefited – at least artistically – from the Second. His cartoon subjects and even his sense of humour of the inter-war years are gradually sinking into the mulch of nostalgia and the carnage of class-warfare. But his wartime posters seem to retain all their pristine vivacity and urgency. 'How carelessly we should have talked during the war but for Fougasse,' as the then Princess Elizabeth remarked.*

BEVIS HILLIER

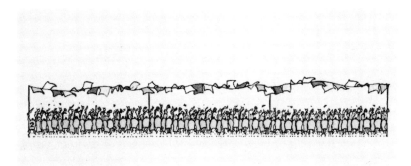

---

* Quoted by Ernest O. Hauser, 'The British Think It's Funny', *Saturday Evening Post*, 28 January 1950, p. 27.

" Gadgets "

"WELL, I'M BLOWED IF I SEE—   —WHAT GOOD—   —I CAN BE—   —TURNING OUT—

—TO FIGHT—   —THEM—   —BLOOMING—   —GERMANS—

—WITH ALL THEIR—   —GUNS—   —AND THEIR MILLIONS O' MEN— . . . .

—AND SO FORTH—   —AND SO ON.   BEEN PREPARING FOR THIS, THEY HAVE,—

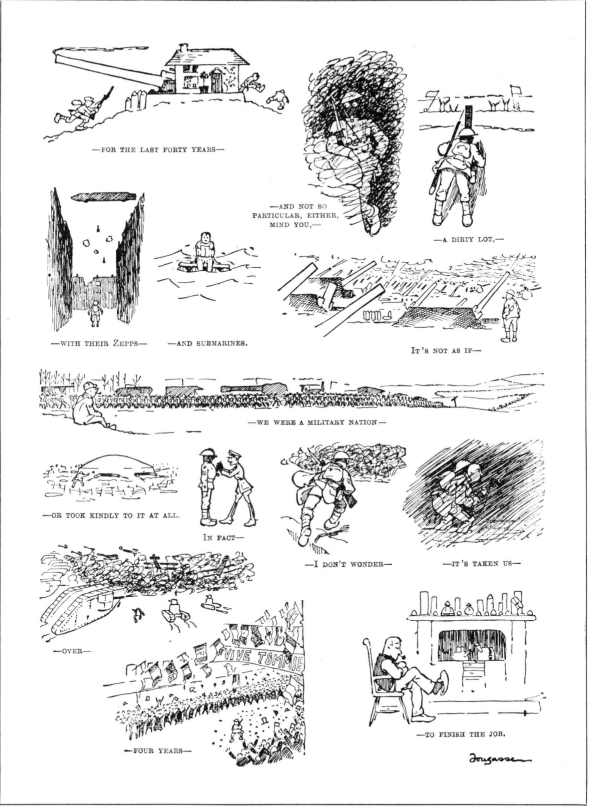

—FOR THE LAST FORTY YEARS—

—AND NOT SO PARTICULAR, EITHER, MIND YOU,—

—A DIRTY LOT,—

—WITH THEIR ZEPPS—

—AND SUBMARINES.

IT'S NOT AS IF—

—WE WERE A MILITARY NATION—

—OR TOOK KINDLY TO IT AT ALL.

IN FACT—

—I DON'T WONDER—

—IT'S TAKEN US—

—OVER—

—FOUR YEARS—

—TO FINISH THE JOB.

Fougasse

1914—1918—II.

THE CHARM OF VILLAGE CRICKET LIES TO A GREAT EXTENT IN THE STRESS IT PLACES ON THE INDIVIDUAL FACTOR. FOR INSTANCE, ONE KNOWS THAT, OTHER THINGS BEING EQUAL, IF ONE HITS THE BALL DIRECTLY TOWARDS A—

Fougasse

FIELDER IN A CLOTH CAP ONE CAN RUN A SINGLE—

AND IF HE'S WEARING BRACES ONE CAN RUN TWO—

BUT IF HE'S GOT ON ONE OF THOSE FANCY SWEATERS ONE STAYS WHERE ONE IS.

SIMILARLY, A BELT WITH A SNAKE IN IT MEANS A SINGLE—

SO DOES A CLUB TIE—

WHEREAS A GENT'S FANCY BOW MEANS TWO.

ONE TAKES NO RISKS, OF COURSE, WITH A HANDKERCHIEF ROUND THE NECK—

BUT ONE GETS IN TWO FOR TROUSERS TUCKED INTO SOCKS—

STRETCHING IT TO THREE FOR A STRAW HAT—

AND FOUR FOR A BLACK WAISTCOAT—

WHILE FOR CUFFS BUTTONED AT THE WRIST—

OR A DICKEY ONE JUST RUNS IT OUT.

WITH SMALL BOYS IN SHORTS ONE NATURALLY TAKES NO CHANCES WHATEVER—   AS EVERYONE KNOWS THEY ARE APT TO BECOME SO CONFOUNDEDLY ENTHUSIASTIC.

THE CHARM OF VILLAGE CRICKET

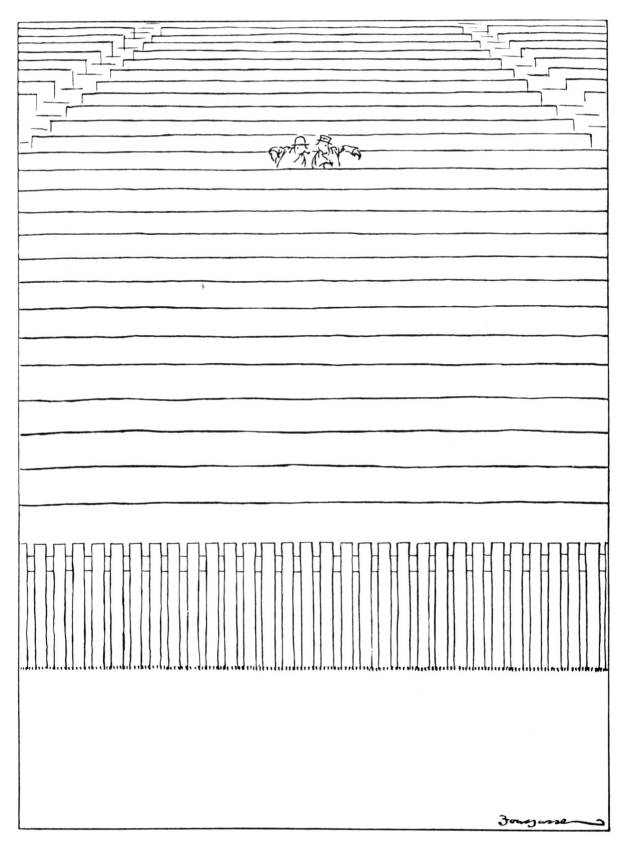

"OF COURSE, THERE'S ONE THING THAT NO FOREIGNER WILL EVER UNDERSTAND, AND THAT'S OUR ENTHUSIASM FOR CRICKET."

SEEING THE REGATTA.

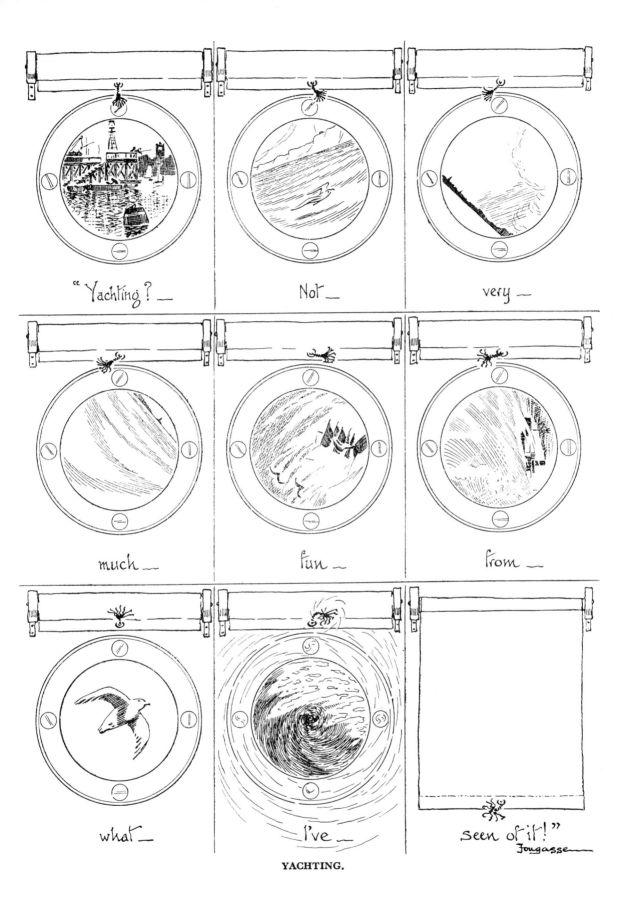

YACHTING.

I don't hold with these ultra-modern fellows as a rule, but I should think they could knock something quite decent out of a Rugger-scrum.

" I'M AFRAID I SHAN'T BE ABLE TO GET ASHORE TO SEE POMPEII TO-MORROW—THERE'S SOME TALK OF PLAYING OFF THE FINAL OF THE DECK-BILLIARDS."

THE INCONSIDERATE BATHER.

OWING TO THE SHORTAGE OF— BATHING-MACHINES AT SHINGLESEA— THE ACTION OF MR. JONES, FROM SEA-VIEW—

IN— GETTING— CARRIED— RIGHT—

OUT— TO SEA— UNTIL—

PICKED UP— BY A PASSING— STEAMER—

CAUSED A GREAT DEAL OF INCONVENIENCE TO OTHER BATHERS.

Fougasse—

"Whenever I use—

one of these—

antiquated bathing machines—

I am always—

irresistibly—

reminded—

of jokes about them—

in the comic papers."

THE SITTER.

"MINE, PARTNER."

eat more TURNIPS
the world's finest food

eat more DATES
the world's finest food

eat more SAGO
the world's finest food

eat more PICKLES
the world's finest food

eat more BUNS
the world's finest food

eat more PARSLEY
the world's finest food

eat more MAIZE
the world's finest food

eat more MANGOES
the world's finest food

eat more NUTS
the world's finest food

THE FIRST DAY OF DOING THEM.

THE FIRST DAY OF SHIRKING THEM.

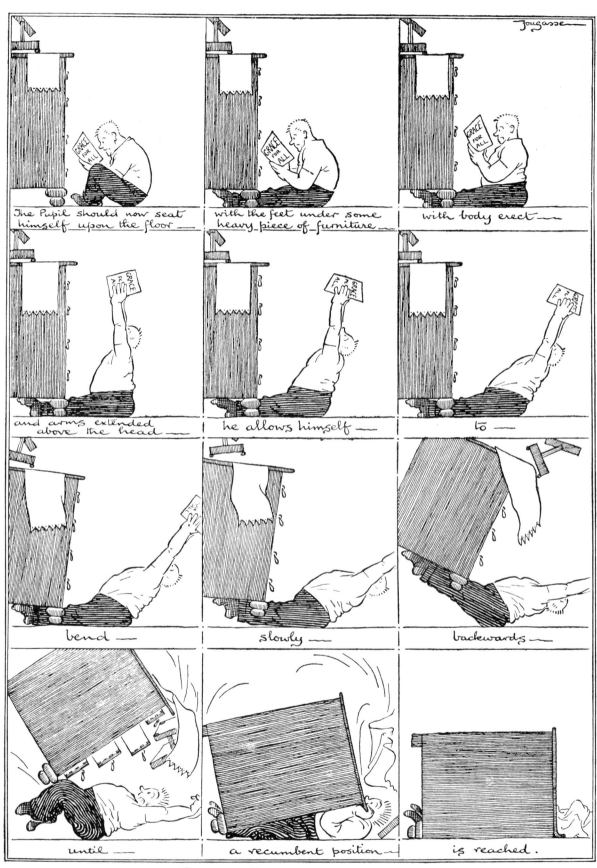

EXERCISE 3.—TO PROMOTE A GRACEFUL FIGURE.

HOPE.

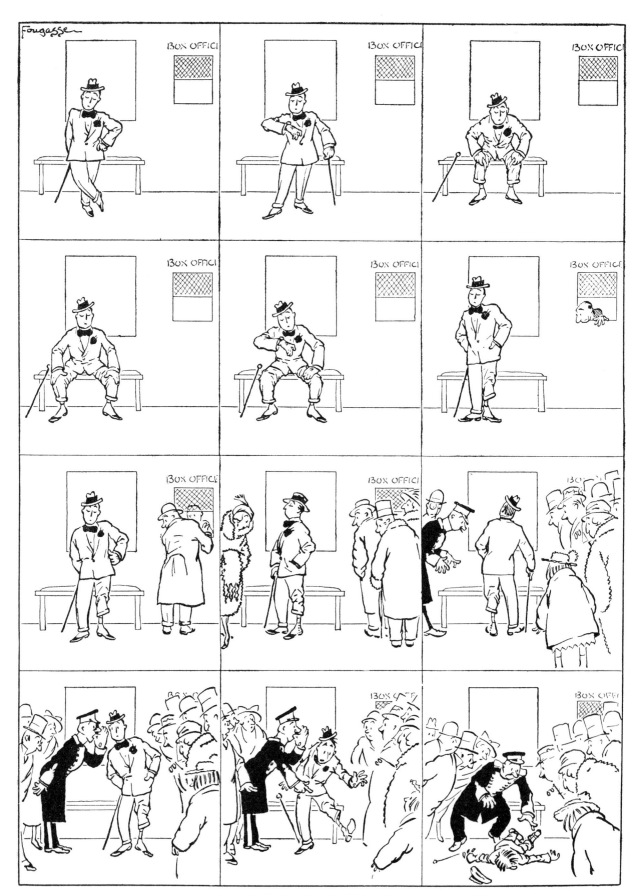

THE TRAGEDY OF A TROUSER

"GOOD HEAVENS, THERE'S A FELLOW IN OXFORD BAGS!"

"GREAT SCOTT, THERE'S A FELLOW NOT IN OXFORD BAGS!"

"POWERS ABOVE, THERE'S A FELLOW STILL IN OXFORD BAGS!"

NIGHTMARE

" Now, you, sir, in the front row of the stalls—let's hear you
sing the chorus by yourself."

DELIGHTS OF A HOTEL LOUNGE

"And what was it you said you were suffering from?"

THE RECOGNITION SCENE

Jorgasse

" How do you do, Mr. Jones ? Now I'm sure you
don't remember who I am ? "

" But of course I do ! How could I have forgotten ? . . . Where are you living now ? Still—
er——"
" Yes, still at the old place. How clever of you
to remember ! "

" Of course I do. . . . And how's—er—everyone ? "
" Oh, they're all very well, thanks. They'll be
delighted you remembered them."

" But naturally I do, perfectly. . . . And what
are you doing these days ? Still— er——"
" Oh, just the same as before. What a memory
you've got ! "

" How could I forget ? It seems no further off than yesterday that we met at—er——"

" No, it doesn't seem any time, does it ? And yet you might so easily have forgotten."

" Oh, rather not, impossible. . . . What times the] were, weren't they ? Down at—er—with the er——"

" Yes, weren't they ? Splendid ! "

" I'll never forget any of it—how we—er—that time we—er—when we—er——"

" No, neither shall I."

" Oh, well, I give it up. Who on earth are you ?

COMICSCRIPTITIS

No, please don't worry—I'm quite all right; I'm only doing this as a slight protest against the conventi[on] that a humorous series must—

START PEACEFULLY—

AND—

LEAD—

GRADUALLY—

UP—

TO—

SOME—

VIOLENT—

CALAMITY.

"WOULD YOU HAVE THE GOODNESS TO STOP TALKING, SIR?"

"I WAS *not* TALKING, SIR."

"WELL, YOU ARE NOW, ANYWAY."

TACT

Fougasse

A PLAIN BIT AT ONE END—

AND A MID-VICTORIAN FIGURE
AT THE OTHER—

AND THEN YOU'VE GOT TO—

TIE IT—

AND PULL IT—

AND TUG AT IT—

AND FIDDLE WITH IT—

UNTIL—

IT LOOKS MUCH MORE LIKE A
MADE-UP TIE THAN A MADE-
UP TIE COULD EVER LOOK."

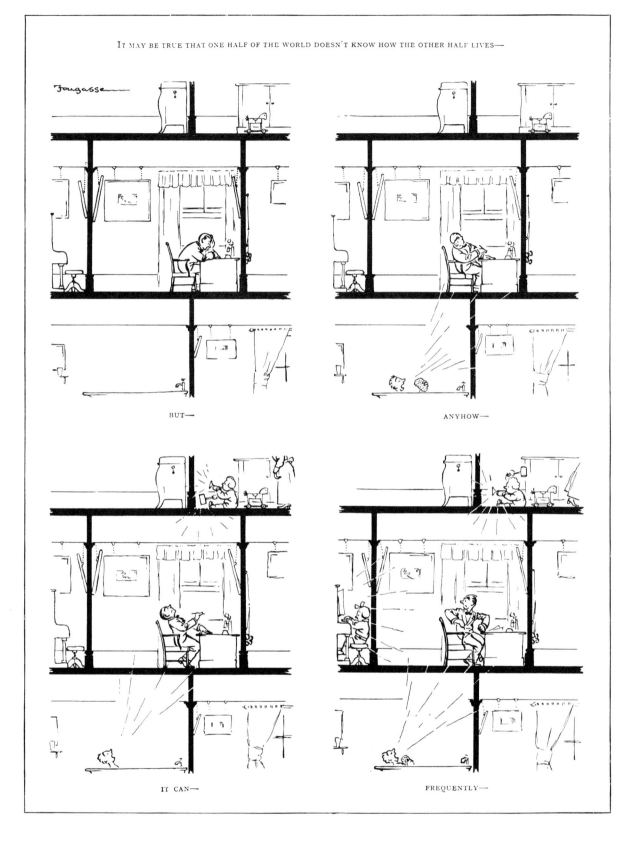

BUT—

ANYHOW—

IT CAN—

FREQUENTLY—

GIVE—

A—

VERY GOOD—

GUESS.

" It's quite all right, my dear fellow. You see, everything has to give way
to a sailing-vessel."

THE LOUD-SPEAKER

ANTICLIMAX.

Fougasse

" Your Excellencies -

Your Graces—

My Lords—

Ladies—

and Gentlemen—

Pray silence—

for the Right Honourable—

Somebody Something,

His Majesty's—

Secretary of State—

for Important Affairs."

". . . Er—Ladies and Gentlemen—

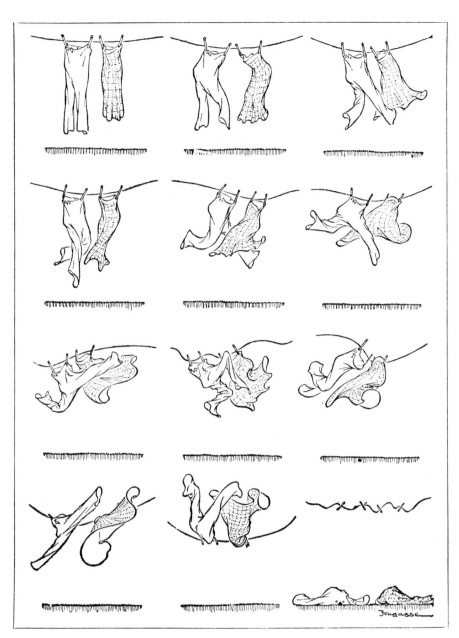

DANSE DES VENTS

Frugasson

FIRST NIGHT.

SECOND NIGHT.

THIRD NIGHT.

FOURTH NIGHT.

FIFTH NIGHT.

SIXTH NIGHT.

"OH, PERCIVAL, HOW DREADFUL! WHEN I SENT THAT PICTURE POSTCARD TO AUNT LOUISA, I DO
BELIEVE I PUT A CROSS AGAINST THE WRONG WINDOW."

PORTRAIT OF A GENTLEMAN IN PROCESS OF DECIDING THAT THE HIRE OF A CAR TO TAKE HIM TO HIS FANCY-DRESS REVEL WOULD HAVE BEEN WELL WORTH THE EXPENSE.

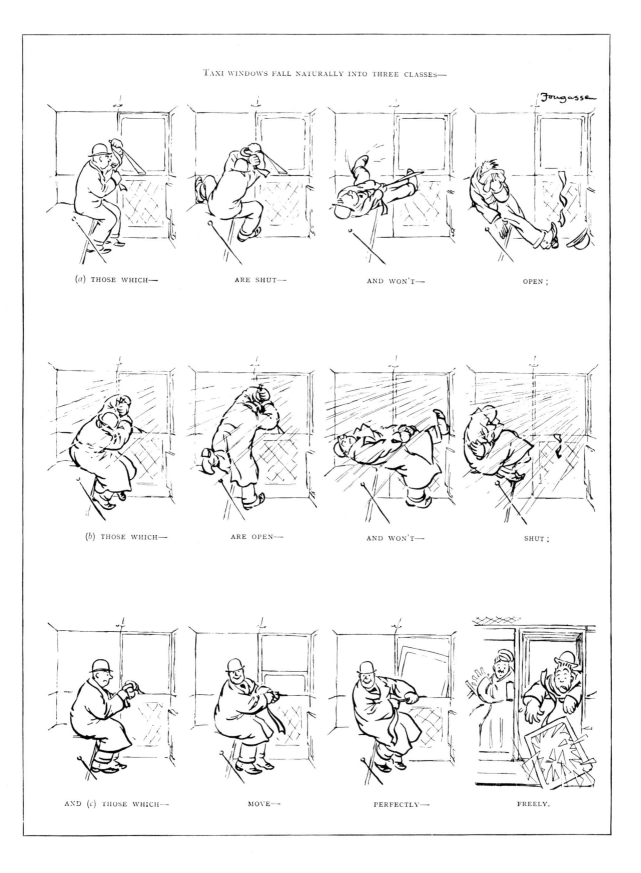

" Well, *I can't* think what's given me the 'ump this morning."

"DID YOU RING, SIR?"
"YES; THERE'S A WASP IN THE ROOM."

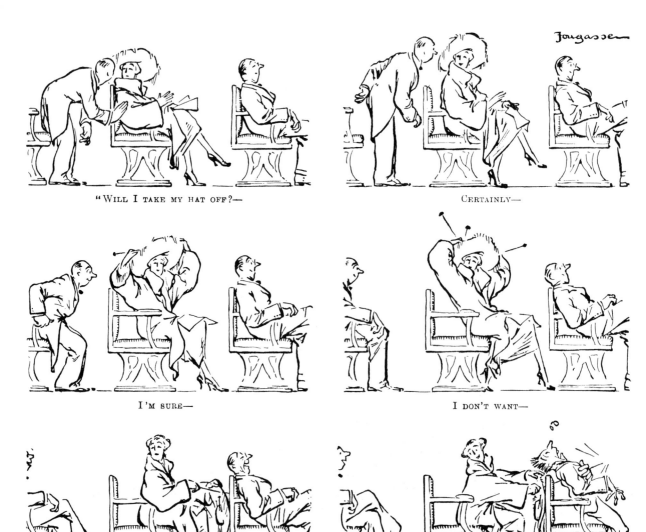

"WILL I TAKE MY HAT OFF?—

CERTAINLY—

I'M SURE—

I DON'T WANT—

TO BE A NUISANCE—

TO ANYBODY."

" And now may we see some a little thicker still—unless the rain's stopped ? "

Brr—

" Hullo. . . . Oh, is that *you*, darling ? . . . how *lovely* to hear
your voice, my sweet . . .

What ? . . . Oh, my *dear*, how *marvellous* ! . . . that's *quite*
the most *wonderful* news I've had for *years* . . .

Darling, I'm *thrilled* . . . yes . . . yes . . . what ? . . . *what* ?
. . . nonsense ! . . . it *can't* be *true* ! ! ! . . .

But how *simply* too *terrible* for *words* ! ! ! . . . no . . . yes . . .
yes . . . no . . . *my dear*, I can't *believe* it ! ! ! . . .

Yes, *awful* . . . no, *ghastly* . . . yes, *horrible*. No, it's just *too
perfectly frightful* ! ! ! . . . Good-night, my sweet . . . good-
night . . .

It was only that tiresome Brown-Robinson girl—

No news, as usual—just wanted a bit of a chat."

" Is that you, dear ? I rang you up because I wanted to ask you something in a great hurry. . .

Can you hear me, dear ?— Yes, I can hear quite well. . .

Better than last time, I think – I said better than last time. . .

I said I can hear you better. . .

Yes, I can hear quite distinct- ly—perhaps it's something to do with the weather. . .

Yes, the weather. Oh, no, it's been lovely here to-day. . .

Has it ? We haven't had any
rain here. . .

No, to-day was lovely—
specially this morning. . .

I said, ' specially this morning '—the sun was shining—
the sun—yes—shining. . .

What, dear ? Oh, there go the
pips—I simply must ring off. . .

I couldn't *possibly* afford
another three minutes. . .

No. Good-night, dear—
Good-night."

" . . . IS THAT SO, MURIEL ? . . .

. . . OH, HAVE THEY, MURIEL ? . . .

. . . YES, VERY STRANGE, DEAR . . .

. . . NO, DEAR . . .

. . . YES, DEAR . . .

. . . YES . . . NO . . . YES . . .

. . . NO . . . YES . . . NO . . .

. . . YES. AND DO *you* KNOW THAT THE BODY OF OLD SILAS MUGGRIDGE HAS BEEN FOUND IN THE SCULLERY AT No. 15 IN A POOL OF BLOOD ? . . .

THAT IRIS MAINWARING WENT OUT TO POST A LETTER AT 7.25 P.M. AND *never returned ?* . . .

THAT THE GROUNDSEL IN THE CAGE OF MADAME GRENADINE'S CANARY WAS FOUND TO CONTAIN THIRTY-FIVE PER CENT OF GUN-COTTON, AND THAT INSPECTOR BEAGLE HAS JUST ARRESTED HORACE FEATHERSTONE ?—

WHAT—WHO ARE THEY ALL ?—

WHY, THE CHARACTERS IN THE BOOK I'M ATTEMPTING TO READ, OF COURSE."

THE POSTER WHICH JONES GOT OUT FOR SEAVILLE WAS PERHAPS A LITTLE TOO STRIKING FOR SOME TASTES. I'M AFRAID, HOWEVER, THAT THE—

TOWN COUNCIL'S AMENDMENT DID RATHER SPOIL ITS APPEAL.

"WILL I DINE WITH YOU ON FRIDAY? . . .

MAY I RUN UPSTAIRS AND LOOK AT MY BOOK? . . .

. . . . . .

. . . . . .

. . . . . .

. . . . . .

. . . . . .

. . . . . .

. . . . . .

. . . . . .

. . . . . .

FRIGHTFULLY SORRY; I FIND I'M ENGAGED."

SMITH, LEARNING TO DRIVE IN HIS NEW CAR, ARRIVES OPPORTUNELY AT A SMASH-AND-GRAB RAID,
AND IS BIDDEN TO "FOLLOW THAT CAR AND GO LIKE HELL!"

THE HORN THAT STUCK—I

THE HORN THAT STUCK—II

"HULLO, IS THAT POLICE? THEN I WONDER IF YOU COULD POSSIBLY TELL ME OF A WORD IN TEN LETTERS, OF WHICH THE FIRST IS 'B,' THE SECOND 'L,' THE FIFTH 'B,' AND THE SEVENTH 'T,' MEANING A SLANG TERM FOR A POLICEMAN?"

"I SAY, I'M MOST AWFULLY SORRY—HONESTLY, I QUITE THOUGHT YOU WERE CHAUFFEURS."

REVERSION IN TYPE

" The Daily Blot's " photograph of Sir X. S. Proffit at his riverside residence
was an excellent likeness of the great man ; but, all the same, it was a singu-
larly tactless mistake to publish it the wrong way up.

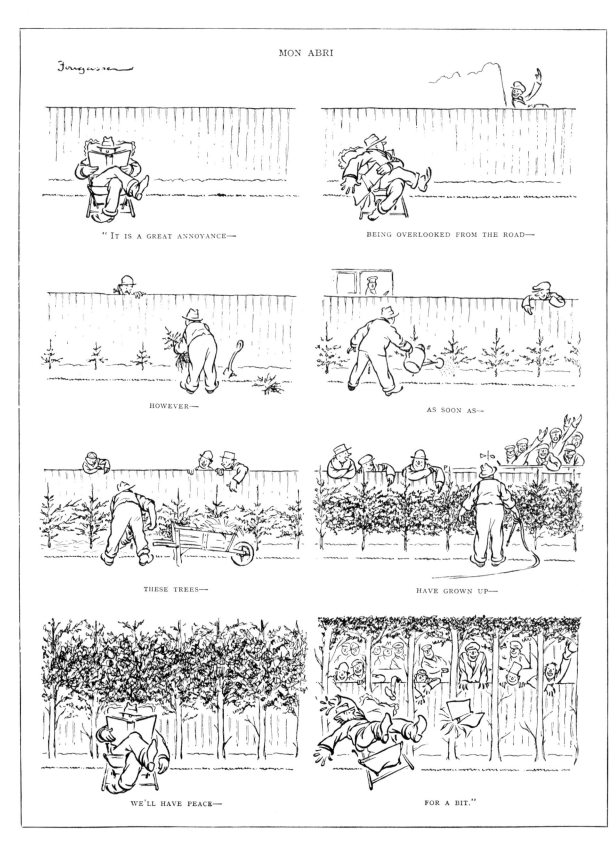

" No, I refused to be bought out ; you see, I was fond of the place and its surroundings."

THE FIR-WOODS USED TO COME RIGHT DOWN TO OUR VILLAGE.

NOW, OF COURSE, THEY'VE COME RIGHT DOWN INTO IT.

THE ROBINSONS' HOUSE USED TO BE SOME DISTANCE AWAY ACROSS THE FIELDS.

NOW IT'S ONLY JUST ACROSS THE ROAD.

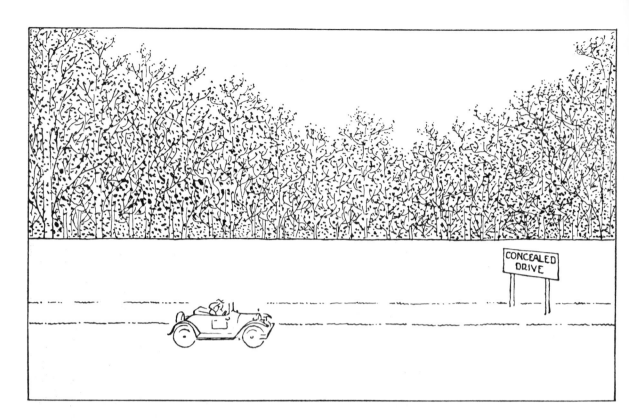

MODESTY

Jougasse

THE SENTIMENTALIST

Citizen—1

Citizen—2

Citizen—3

Citizen—4

The Lost Ticket

Fougasse

"Stop! Stop!! I—forgot—to—put—my—ticket—in—your—litterbox!!!"

Help us save paper

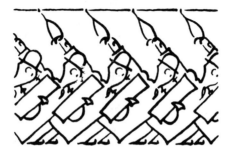

Rush-hour.

Taking the Plunge ?

If your age is
between 14 and 18 why not go and see the local Secretary
of The National Association of Training Corps for Girls at

_____

GO AS SOON AS YOU CAN: YOU'LL FIND IT'S WELL WORTH IT

The little noise, & how much it can be.

NOISE
ALMOST ALWAYS ANNOYS

"I'm afraid you'll have to shout — I make so much noise I can't hear a thing."

CLATTER
DOES MATTER

"Heavens, no — I wouldn't tell a soul!"

CARELESS TALK
COSTS LIVES

SPECIALLY DRAWN AND PRINTED FOR THE AMERICAN RED CROSS IN GREAT BRITAIN

Don't forget that walls have ears!

CARELESS TALK COSTS LIVES

"........ but for Heaven's sake
don't say I told you!"

CARELESS TALK
COSTS LIVES